Life after Retirement

....

Steve Brown

New Growth Press

WWW.NEWGROWTHPRESS.COM

New Growth Press, Greensboro, NC 27404
www.newgrowthpress.com
Copyright © 2015 by Steve Brown

Cover Design: Faceout Books, faceoutstudio.com
Typesetting: Lisa Parnell, lparnell.com

ISBN: 978-1-942572-22-0 (Print)
ISBN: 978-1-942572-23-7 (eBook)

Library of Congress Cataloging-in-Publication Data
Brown, Stephen W.
  Life after retirement / Steve Brown.
     pages cm
   ISBN 978-1-942572-22-0 (print) —
   ISBN 978-1-942572-23-7 (ebook)
1. Retirees—Religious life. I. Title.
 BV4596.R47B76 2015
 248.8'5—dc23
                                                     2015001510

Printed in China

25 24 23 22 21 20 19 18   2 3 4 5 6

O God, from my youth you have taught me,
and I still proclaim your wondrous deeds.
So even to old age and gray hairs,
O God, do not forsake me,
until I proclaim your might to another generation,
your power to all those to come.
Psalm 71:17–18

I have a deep, resonant, and youthful-sounding voice. Because much of what I do is on radio and audio CDs, people have a skewed idea of the way I look. Most expect the Marlboro man so when people meet me, they're shocked. Once when I was speaking in St. Louis, a young man told me he came because he wanted to see what I looked like. "Dr. Brown," he said, "you're old!" As he walked away he looked back and said, "I mean really old!"

Frankly, I've looked old much of my life. Most of my hair is gone and has been for a long time. What hair I have left, along with my beard, is white and started turning white when I was in my forties. (Think Santa and you're close.) I used to joke to my congregation, "You did this to me. I didn't look this way when I came here. But I will have the last laugh. You're going to turn old and I'll watch . . . but I'm going to look this way until I die."

But now I'm as old as dirt and the reality has merged with the image. It's one thing to look old and quite another to be old. Now that I'm really old and should be retired, what should I do? If you're old, let me give you some biblical thoughts that helped me. I have some questions and at least a hint of some answers for us.

Perhaps you're retired and living a totally different life than you did when you worked nine-to-five, and this isn't what you expected. Perhaps you're a golfer, but now that you have time to play golf, it isn't as much fun as it was when you had to fight for the time to play. Perhaps you have a second career and it isn't working for you. Perhaps you're going through the "empty nest syndrome," and the longing and quiet make the days really hard. Some of you are struggling with significant physical limitations and whatever works hurts. Could be you're reading books you didn't have time to read when you were younger or watching a lot more television, and getting bored with both . . . or not. Maybe you've lost loved ones and friends, and a "what's the use . . . we all die" attitude has set in while your favorite book of the Bible has become Ecclesiastes. Maybe you, like me, wince at the changes that have taken place in you and in the world, and you don't like them at all.

Then again, maybe you're perfectly happy with your old age. If you are, I personally think you're a fruitcake. But if you are (i.e., happy and a fruitcake), you shouldn't read any further.

The truth is that all old people have one thing in common: we struggle with significance. A retired executive once approached my late mentor, Fred Smith, and said, "Fred, when I was in business, I had a lot of buttons on my desk and when I pushed any one of them, something happened. Now I don't have one d—— button." That's a metaphor for all of us. Things have changed with age, and now that there aren't any "buttons," who am I and does it even matter?

Question: What do I do now?

Answer: The same thing you have always done, even if now a bit slower and smarter.

The psalmist said to God, "O God, from my youth you have taught me, and I still proclaim your wondrous deeds" (Psalm 71:17). In other words, I'm doing what I've always done and I'll keep on doing it until I die. What is that? It is "proclaim[ing] your [God's] might to another generation, your power to all those to come" (v. 18).

Jesus said to "go into all the world and proclaim the gospel to the whole creation" (Mark 16:15). A proper translation of that is "*as you are going* into all the world." Add to that Paul's comment that Christians are the "aroma of Christ" (2 Corinthians 2:15), and we have a clear commission from God that tells us what to do in our lives before and after retirement.

That hasn't changed. As we go wherever it is we go and as we do whatever it is we do, we "smell like Jesus." The gospel of God's love and mercy hasn't changed and the representatives of that gospel shouldn't either.

Following the funeral for her 92-year-old husband, the funeral director asked a widow about her age. "I'm 89," she said. "It's hardly worth the effort to go home." As we get older, it's easy to think, "It's hardly worth the effort." One of the differences between being young and being old is that when you're young, you have to show up. There are thousands of obligations that simply have to be met. We don't have to show up anymore, and it's a temptation not to.

I have a friend who describes life as a series of plateaus to which one climbs, rests, and then heads for the next one. He says, "When you reach a plateau, quit climbing, and run around in circles, you're old." We may climb slower than we did and we probably have to be more careful in the climbing, but we can't stop showing up for the next climb. When we don't show up, we die; we just haven't been buried yet.

I work for a ministry founded to proclaim "radical freedom, infectious joy, and surprising faithfulness" in different formats. I record syndicated teaching programs and talk shows on radio, teach seminars, produce books and videos, and speak and teach in a great variety of venues. The problem is that I'm getting older. Well . . . I am old.

Our board once felt that when I could no longer do it, we would shut down the ministry and be thankful for what God had done and that we had not lost too many. But, as of late, our board decided that the message of God's grace and the way we deliver it ought to continue after I'm no longer around. To that end, we've brought into Key Life a number of young, gifted, and committed folks whose ministries are being used by God in significant and exciting ways. If I died tomorrow, there would be some problems, but if I can hold on for a while, Key Life will survive and thrive.

So in a joking way our entire board and staff are preparing for "D. D. day"—the day Steve drools or dies. I'm cramming for finals and I know that day is coming, but until then, with the psalmist, I can say to God, "You've always been there from my youth and I still proclaim your wondrous deeds."

For those of us who are Christians, that proclamation still defines us no matter where we go or what we do.

Question: How do I do it?

Answer: The way Jesus did.

Someone has said that old people are already irritated about being old so it takes very little to tick them off. There's some truth to that, but if you're a Christian, the Holy Spirit is at work.

One of the most important books I've read in years was Henri Nouwen's *The Return of the Prodigal Son: A Story of Homecoming*.[1] That was such a good book, but there was one thing in it that changed my life. It was the recognition that the father loved both of his sons the same. One was a hell-raiser who messed up his life, and the other was a self-righteous twit who made everybody (including himself) miserable. I see myself in both of those sons. Nouwen reminded me that when I see it in others, I should respond in the same way that my heavenly Father responded to me. Then Nouwen reminded me that the father in the parable is given as an example to the old of the gift we are to give to the young. The father in the parable gave grace, love, and mercy to both of his sons, and neither one of them deserved it.

One of the things I've noticed lately is the way young and beautiful women react to me. I once did a television show out of New York. When the director and I first met, she said, "Steve, you're ugly, but your face has character." I'm okay with that, but character isn't what's attractive to the opposite sex. Recently, though, I've noticed that young women seem to be flirting with me. That's a new experience. I was surprised and, frankly, quite pleased until a friend told me, "Steve, are you crazy? They're not flirting with you. They think you're their grandfather!"

That grandfather thing has become more and more a reality in my relationships. I've noticed that people cut me slack they didn't before, are kinder than they were, and are less offended by what I say. Not only that, I have freedom I never had before because there isn't any leverage over me.

I have a friend, John Frost, who helps us create and produce Think Spots, one-minute commentaries on a variety of subjects, which air on a number of radio stations across the country. John is a hard taskmaster, directing me as I record those spots and often requiring me to do multiple versions over and over again. It's quite frustrating and sometimes I get irritated and say things I shouldn't. After one long day of recording and some anger, John said to me, "Steve, I finally have you figured out. You don't care."

I decided he's right. Of course I care about some things, but I don't care much what people think about me, which celebrities are sleeping together, or who is tweeting whom. And I don't have to prove anything to anybody, I don't have to be right, and I don't have to defend anything. Add to that the fact that the bills are paid, I'm not looking for a job, and I'm perfectly happy with my wife of fifty-three years. It has dawned on me that I've been given a gift. It's called freedom—a freedom I never experienced when I was young. It is freedom that will make me either a malediction or a benediction (a curse or a blessing).

I teach at a seminary and I've noticed that it's the nature of the young to be quite harsh and self-righteous in their judgments of heresy and sin. (I often wish I knew as much as they know.) Mostly, I respond by smiling and trying to ignore it, recognizing that they will grow up just as I did. But sometimes, when the students become insufferable, I say, "Boys, you haven't lived long enough or sinned big enough to even have an opinion on that subject."

One of the good things about being old (and there aren't many of them) is that we've lived long enough and we've sinned big enough to know that anything we are, anything we have, and anything of importance in our lives has come as a gift of God's grace. When you're old (more than at any other time in your life), if you choose, you can give the same gift to others. In fact, I believe that's the commission God gives to those of us who are old. We are called to be like the father in the parable of the prodigal son. This doesn't mean we never acknowledge sin, but we do so without condemnation and with arms open wide to receive even the worst sinner.

Question: If I take the psalmist seriously, what should I expect?
Answer: God's continuing grace!

When you're cramming for finals, the great danger is to try to fix what is broken, remedy the failure, and make up for the sin. If you try to do that (and I have), there is great frustration. First, you will spend all of your time trying to please God and others. If you're a Christian, God is already pleased, and the others need a witness more than an effort to fix you or them. That's what the psalmist discovered. He said he wanted to "proclaim your [God's] might to another generation, your power to all those to come."

As you know, the trademark of the shoe company Nike is "Just Do It!" That, of course, can get you into trouble if you do really stupid things. But what if you decided to go out in a blaze of glory, to say what you never had the courage to say before, to love people you never loved before, to go places you always wanted to go, and to make sure that everybody you know hears about God and his grace? What if you decided to build a house for the poor, to be a missionary to a country that needs you, or to work in the church that has nurtured you? What if you were willing?

We'll never do it right, there will always be problems, and we'll still struggle with sin and doubt (we're not home yet), but we could be God's gift to the young. It's a rare gift in a fallen world—a gift of honesty (we don't have to pretend anymore), authenticity (who we are defines us), and love (one can't love until one has been loved, and then only to the degree that one has been loved—and we've been loved big).

The truth is that, if you look around, there are plenty of places to go, people to see, and things to do in the name of Christ. In fact, if you ask him, God will open all kinds of doors. You'll feel like a mosquito in a nudist colony—you'll know what to do but have trouble deciding where to start.

That would be fun. Really. Just do it!

Question: That sounds big. The problem is that I'm not good enough and I don't know enough. Who am I to do this?

Answer: You are an adopted son or daughter of the King of the Universe.

The problem here is significance, so here's the real question: How do you deal with your significance when the world has passed you by, when you're simply tired of trying, and when you wonder if anything matters? If you belong to Jesus, you deal with significance the same way you did when you were young. You don't define yourself by *what* you do, but by *who* you are.

Augustine said, "If you want to be great, be."

One of the good things about being old is that you have a "nonsense meter." That gift will give you a view of yourself and the world that is quite satisfying—as long as you don't let it make you cynical. You grow tired of the lies and the drivel. Dr. House (of television fame) says, "Everybody lies." While I don't agree with that completely, there is some truth to it, and the older I get the more I can tell. Age gives you perspective on what's true and what isn't, what's important and what isn't, and what one should care about and what doesn't matter.

A publisher once asked me to write a new introduction to a book I had written some twenty-five years before. It was an interesting experience. The book was a manual of basic Christian doctrine for new Christians, originally written during the Jesus Movement when so many new Christians were coming into the church. As I wrote the new introduction, I had a copy of the original book on my desk—with my photo on the back cover.

I looked at the photo of the young man on the book jacket and thought, *You were so young then . . . Your dreams were so big. Nothing was impossible. You were going to win the world to Christ.*

I became quite aware that a whole lot had happened since I wrote that book. I had faced the tragedy of unfulfilled dreams and the fact that I wasn't nearly as righteous or as knowledgeable as I thought I was. As I looked at my old photo, I thought about the years of work and ministry, the babies I buried, the confessions I heard, the deathbeds I stood by, and the suicides I cleaned up. I thought about the heartbreak I experienced, the loved ones I lost, the people I hurt, and the times I was not as faithful as I should have been. As I looked at that young man in the photo, I remembered that he was whole then. I became aware of the armor that now has chinks in it. I thought of how often my heart was broken and how, over the years, I learned to love more and maybe question more.

But that sounds so bleak.

It hasn't all been that way—not by any means. As I thought of the years that had passed, I remembered the good things. I thought of my family, the great number of people God allowed me to know and love, the work, and my full life. A lot of the lines in my face are now laugh lines. I'm old now and the years have presented me with a gift of being less concerned about what people will say and think about me, and more concerned with what people think about Jesus.

As I looked at that book, I realized that what I had written years before didn't need a rewrite. Truth is still truth and eternal verities are still the same. The difference is that the truth I wrote about years earlier has gone through many years of testing and is more true to me now than it was at any other time in my life.

The blood of Christ is still sufficient, his righteousness is still imputed to my account, and God's kindness and grace are still amazing.

And I'm going to tell as many people as I can.

Okay, that's all I know about getting old. And I don't want to talk about it anymore.

Endnote

1. Henri J. M. Nouwen, *The Return of the Prodigal Son: A Story of Homecoming* (New York: Doubleday, 1994).

Simple, Quick, Biblical

Advice on Complicated Counseling Issues
for Pastors, Counselors, and Individuals

MINIBOOK
CATEGORIES

- Personal Change
- Marriage & Parenting
- Medical & Psychiatric Issues
- Women's Issues
- Singles
- Military

Are you tired of
"do more, try harder" religion?

Key Life has only one message, to communicate the
radical grace of God to sinners and sufferers.
Because of what Jesus has done, God's not mad at you.

On radio, in print, on CDs and online, we're
proclaiming the scandalous reality of Jesus' good
news of radical grace...leading to radical freedom,
infectious joy and surprising faithfulness to Christ.

For all things grace, visit us at **KeyLife.org**